AF266960

The *Spirit* of *Becoming*

Become a Personal Hero Instead of a
Continual Victim of Circumstance

Leona P. Jackson, B.A.

KP PUBLISHING COMPANY

ISBN: 979-8-9857184-4-7 (Paperback)
ISBN: 979-9-9857184-5-4 (eBook)
Library of Congress Control Number: 2022906031

Editor: Laurel Davis
Cover Design: Juan Roberts
Interior Design: Jennifer Houle
Literary Director: Sandra Slayton James

Published by:

KP Publishing Company
Publisher of Fiction, Nonfiction & Children's Books
Valencia, CA 91355
www.kp-pub.com

Printed in the United States of America

Dedication

Thanks to all of my magnificent heroes, named and un-named.

To name a few:
Parents
Herman and Mattie King

Children
Richard Charles and Secret Charles-Ford

Other Heroes and Sheros
Harriet Tubman

Martin Luther King, Jr.

Oprah Winfrey

President Barack and First Lady Michelle Obama

Freedom Warriors

Writers

Fighters

Critics

Journalists

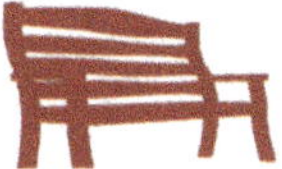

Introduction

The Spirit of Becoming anticipates enlightening the transitional processes concerning physical, emotional, intellectual, social, spiritual, financial, and occupational, mental bench transferring in our thinking, actions, and behavioral mind shifts.

The Spirit of Becoming foretells the saying unquote by John Morley, "No man or woman climbs beyond their psychological or physical limitations alone." I've learned that our bestowed character waits for us to become accountable to some degree or point of willingness. This willingness usually comes from within as a faint but distinct spirit to surrender. Sometimes the act of becoming is simply a decrease in energy to refuse to support the regular abnormal continual tracks of mistrust, doubt, and negativity.

The Spirit of Becoming intends to enhance the sometimes-slow processes between shifts from; unwise to wise, invisible to visible, unsuccessful to successful, chance-taking to choosing, inflexible to resilience, and transforming to transformed.

The Spirit of Becoming gives a mental intrigued tactic while sitting on one bench after another.

Each time we move from bench to bench, it becomes clear that the time spent between turning points is undervalued.

The Spirit of Becoming allowed me to see I had released far more trepidation than I could have imagined all along the way to genuine self-honesty, open-mindedness, willingness, and self-control. Of course, I would hope that others would have supported my humble efforts, but either way, in the end, I became a personal hero instead of a continual victim of circumstance through the Grace of God.

Contents

Part One

Nourishing the Spirit

(Developing)

Benches are used in each chapter as green pastures to meditate on as recipes for a great life, an incredible mental feast.

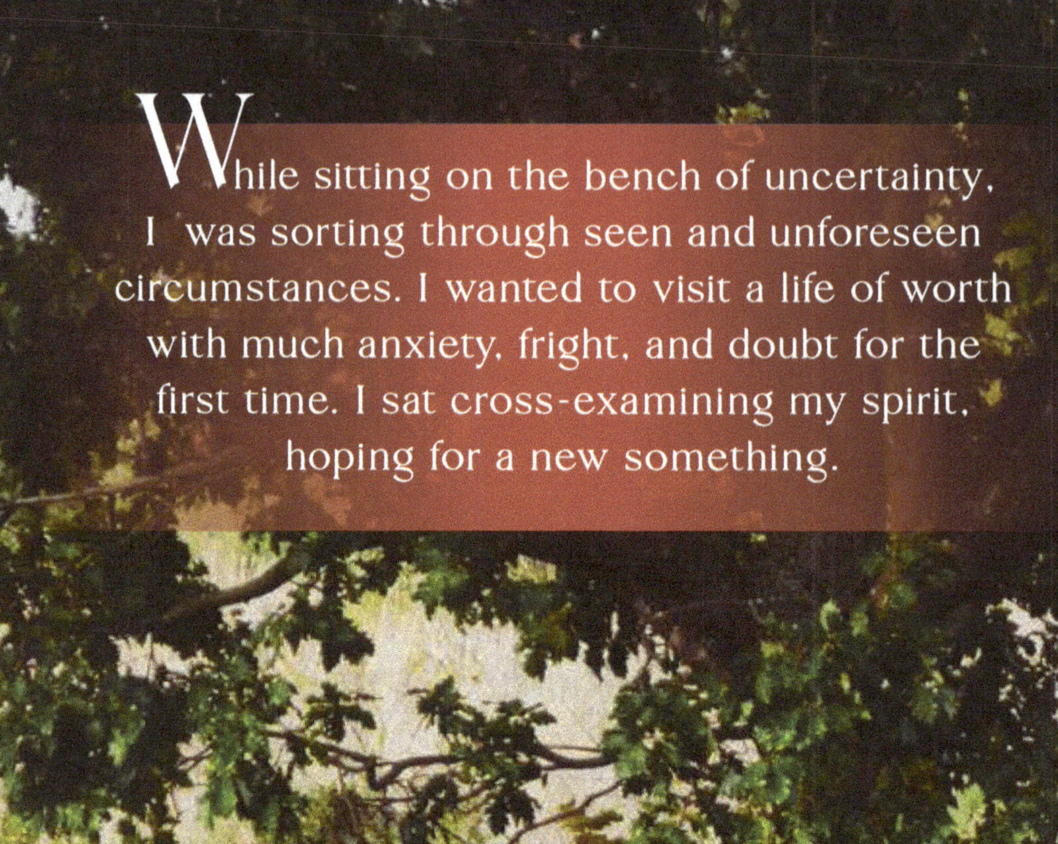

W hile sitting on the bench of uncertainty, I was sorting through seen and unforeseen circumstances. I wanted to visit a life of worth with much anxiety, fright, and doubt for the first time. I sat cross-examining my spirit, hoping for a new something.

1

The Spirit of Struggle

An Element of BELIEF

"Once you learn the true balance of time,
life can be surprisingly different."

—Anonymous

My truth was that I was consciously ashamed of myself starting in 1953. Still, I did not know that was only the beginning of a conscious and unconscious underdeveloped twenty-three-year stronghold clenching tighter and tighter year by year until 1977.

There had always been a hum within me as a small child. I felt the vibes of many known and unknown tunes ever so strong as I tried to wish my mighty circumstances away. But, as life continued, my humming disappeared within the thickness of the unmanageable, uncontrollable, demanding, struggling lifestyle. I believe the spirit of struggle is one of the most profound engines of the process of coming to believe.

At last, I saw, felt, and believed; that eliminating, minimizing, and examining my useless struggles in life was the urgent task at hand.

My first step toward tangible change was sorting through my pointless and worthwhile efforts. The second step was to become willing to see and let go of unnecessary struggles daily. The third step was to learn more from my fundamental challenges.

I had learned to mimic those performing tasks around me and became bombarded with many ineffective habits. Then, one day, I realized patterns of brokenness are to be revisited, repaired, and relinquished.

Sometimes I intuitively felt a few wholesome traits about me; however, my instincts did not have a fighting chance due to excessive fear, doubt, and panic. As a result, I could not articulate those traits early on. I even struggled not to let go of my unidentified strengths at a young age. I had an energy and an insight that was unstoppable. I was a great laborer beyond my understanding.

I could weather most family business storms unafraid. But, by the time I realized building on my strengths was permissible, my promising powers had vanished—abilities like devotion, determination, and dedication. Whining was not my master then. Instead, I spent time hiding, dismissing, or disowning my new forming weaknesses, which required my full attention.

The unknown character traits that could someday make me a person of character had slipped away unannounced. I started rebuilding, reassembling, and reestablishing my core values, presence, and uniting character-building processes at thirty years of age.

I seemed to struggle with every facet of my life: from separating my unsavory behaviors to studying and borrowing the wholesome behaviors of others, communicating, making small talk, and upgrading my self-talk. Improving my financial management hassles was a struggle without conceivable reconstruction. And the quiet and loud desperation and slipping in and out of panic attacks seemed without an end. This quote from Langston Hughes' poem *Mother to Son* says it all when it comes to the struggles of my life: "Life for me ain't been no crystal stair."

I was born and raised in a family where struggling was first nature. Struggling in the early 1950s was a way of life. For a long time, I believed the spirit of struggle was an inherited neurotic sensation. As a family, we were constantly in the hustle and bustle of surviving. Life never got better as I look back; I somehow learned to adjust to the lifestyle's unpleasant, obnoxious, and unacceptable madness. At some point, the ability to survive became my primary purpose. My father always hired extra help to assist with the cumbersome, improper, ill-managed, and mismanaged family business.

As child laborers, my siblings and I were not on the payroll. We lived with the bare necessities. We had a roof over our heads, although sometimes the roof was the top of hauling trucks. Despite our hard work most of our childhood, working utilities were still limited for most of our youth. The callous, harsh, and repetitive shoveling of ditch-digging labor was requested by my father more than a few times for some of my siblings and me. At times, the shovels were taller than us kids. Additional fixable and non-fixable repairs reoccurred back-to-back.

Although we owned five homes, electric power was a shared accommodation when one house or another lacked electrical benefits. Extension cords were connected next door or across the alley where utilities were still in service. Unpaid electric bills seemed to produce more visible and invisible hardships. It was candles for lighting, connecting and disconnecting propane tanks for cooking, and unloading chunks of coal for our new coal stove for heating, which finally ended with the fire department coming to our rescue once.

I was restless, irritable, and discontented throughout my life. Struggling became a lifestyle nuisance. Trying to understand, fit in and belong, and let go of learned dysfunctions were constant and unpleasant battles to endure daily without a physical or emotional map.

Before turning thirty, my purpose was to find an easier way to live. Once I turned thirty, I had to redefine my life goals. I accepted the now-known fact that life will not always be easy. While struggling to find my life purpose, I experimented with remedies I could embrace. Somewhere along the way, physically relocating was always my answer. I relocated many times before realizing this moving back and forth was a mad rut of not knowing how to settle down. I used to relocate every time unpredictable situations appeared. My problematic conditions were primarily mental. Making poor choices was a continuum without any thought.

Finally, I had to surrender that my anxious disposition would not render me any long-term peace of mind. My anxiousness was a learned behavior from the overindulging maddening family routine choice cycles. We were never still, always returning, getting ready to go, or gone. It was like, "On your mark. Get set. Go!" from ages six to sixteen. The first real overall glimpse at my truth was at age seventeen. I surrendered to that "Aha!" moment in time but continued to relocate as a solution. I accepted that I could not stop relocating at twenty-five.

My last restless relocating attack happened in 1977. This time, I surrendered to the problem of relocating and put forth a conscious effort to steady myself, even if only temporarily. But first, I had to consider the possibility of drinking being an enabling factor to the excessive pattern of relocating at will.

I did not have a mental solution; therefore, I relocated physically. However, to aid the trying situation somewhat, I did take a notion to look up three possible causes of my unsteady mental mess in the Diagnostic Statistical Manual of Mental Disorders (DSM-IV). They were bipolar, schizophrenia, and personality disorders. Fortunately, or unfortunately, the only new information I learned from my hasty research was that all three overlapped in symptoms and side effects. Nevertheless, I owned all three and kept moving forward; by this time, I knew that no matter the cause, I had to find a way out.

Once the global Coronavirus pandemic struck in March 2020, the government called for a worldwide shutdown. The virus is called COVID-19. Everyone had to wear a mask and practice social distancing. The pandemic solved a lot of the petty challenges. My peace of mind soared to a higher level of understanding. We finally stopped wearing the masks in June 2021 for a short while and returned to wearing the masks again in August of 2021.

Life is funny with its many twists and turns, but once we recognize that the curves and bends sometimes do not break our spirit. We begin to trust life more and continue to move forward. But first, I had to learn how to stabilize my life and eliminate some of the unnecessary struggles. My many hurdles originated from within and manifested in my behavior, which stimulated my vicious obsession with relocating, thinking, drinking, fearing, and doubting. Yet, there was sometimes a brief, fleeting moment of stillness after each storm.

I had to learn to see past the turbulences of uncertainty; I stopped moving around so much and looked inside to see if I could make the necessary mandatory actions for change to occur. I had to be willing to learn the lessons that life was trying to teach me.

Once I surrendered to the idea that life would always be topsy turvy, I could see some satisfaction in my growth and developmental processes. Much later, many of my problems became foundational gifts in the end. When I begin to make decisions and not allow my difficulties to create my choices, I can now see, feel, and believe differently. I am learning that my gifts are what I do best with the least effort. For example, I could figure out how to live without allowing life's daily challenges to take the lead in my everyday occurrences, as I had witnessed early on.

Accepting and behaving within a solution-based lifestyle was option number one. Option number two was to continue the same unproductive patterns that produced more disorder, chaos, and stress.

If I did not like how my life was going—and I did not—I could change the learning curves. Instead of running from the lyrics thrown at me, I can change the music. I finally learned that songs have impactful, uncompromising consequences. Like the song, *Ain't too Proud to Beg*, by the tempting Temptations. In 1966, I was too proud to beg and stubborn to ask for help. Instead, I began to dedicate more time to accepting my truth. My truth was what it was: the struggles of life would multiply if I kept running blindly instead of facing the many chaotic situations. Finally, I learned to wisely choose my battles that I could change and let go of the many preset conflicts of interest I could not change.

While learning to strengthen my ability to be present, knowing the developmental trajectory I might experience was helpful. One of my favorite models for gaining mastery in something new is Abraham Maslow's *Four Stages of Learning*, which are:

1. *Unconscious Incompetence:* You don't know what you don't know.
2. *Conscious Incompetence:* You know what you don't know.
3. *Conscious Competence:* You have learned what you need to know, but you're ultra-conscious of your new behavior and need to "think" about how to do it.
4. *Unconscious Competence:* The new skill has become ingrained in your brain; you don't have to think about doing it: it comes naturally.

Understanding this model was helpful when I was unfamiliar with learning, relearning, and developing new learning curves.

I have always wanted to look within and start the process of inner healing and renewal. No one had told me there was a process that prepares one to make renewal possible, called "letting go." There is also a process that makes receiving new and different results possible to embrace. Another process is needed to practice building strategies of newly acquired information. Most effective processes are not overnight matters.

One of my decisions was to join a team of healthy, vibrational persons who could feed me non-conflicting information concerning personal and professional enhancement skills. When I listen to positive energy directed toward someone else, threads of that energy soothingly and quietly seep into my gentle spirit. Today, I know that changing my attitude, expectancy, and perspectives are instant problem solvers. I've learned that remaining a victim of my circumstances is a choice—not a punishment. Refusing to change the things I can change only multiplies the useless challenges and allows me to intentionally or unintentionally ignore the essential hard work required to enhance change. Letting go of the things I could not change became a new and different process of gaining knowledge.

I no longer spend days, weeks, months, and even years only focusing on changing the unchangeable; many things have changed today. My views of my harsh childhood memories have finally become gifts of endurance. My core values, feelings of worthiness, and integrity no longer give way to unannounced, time-consuming predicaments.

After I noticed that tripping over what I could not change was the leading cause of many unnecessary struggles, the power to change my struggling processes appeared. Sometimes the new energy appeared in a spark, a flicker, or flash. The ability to intentionally unite intuition, integrity, and inspiration became an internal curriculum process. I began to have less ongoing, drawn-out, useless pandemonium. I finally realized I am an imperfect woman striving to serve a perfect God!

Now, I know there is a time to struggle and not allow what could cause me to panic, inviting the energy of chaos. I have learned to define and redefine my expectations, primarily. One day I decided to pay attention to where I needed to elevate my mindset to eliminate the current and reoccurring cycles, patterns, and relentless struggles. Also, I learned that growth could not occur to its highest potential of excellence later in life without some action. And for the most part, some potential struggles could be eliminated if one chooses to ignore, let go, or not become emotionally engaged with every thought that skates through the mind or lights on the pathway.

It now seems strange to finally be at peace in my everyday life successes. That peace has come by simply having a reservoir of energy to challenge fundamental misunderstandings, having the wisdom to know when to reject useless muddles, and being willing to challenge short- and long-term situational situations.

The natural uplift in my day-to-day experiences has grown. I'm learning that life can be beautiful even with its downs. I've had to forgive many people who were just as broken as I but perhaps did not know they required fixing. But, on the other hand, I've always known I was unhealed. (a fixing). Like Shonda Rhimes said, "The hum came back." That is my story; my hum returned in 1977; it's the hum of love.

What was your last successful struggle?

While benched, my soul sometimes
searched for feelings of serenity,
achievement, and accomplishment; often,
emptiness seemed natural and normal.
Yet, I longed for refills of spirit.

2

The Spirit of Hunger

A segment of DELIGHT

"I wanted a pat on the back from way back!"
—ANONYMOUS

I was a tad bit anxious about going to school on the first day of kindergarten. I was hungry for something at that early age. I quickly found out it was not going to school. I was terrified beyond words. But, the spirit of hunger did not identify why I felt so starved. Going to school could have been a delight, but I was displeased about going from the beginning of 1953 to 1964.

I remember coming home from my half-day kindergarten class. My mother had been my babysitter, but now she had joined the outside hauling business with my father. My mother invited me to climb into one of the three large trucks for the afternoon work shift.

Fast forward seven years, I was now in the sixth grade. I was absent from the classroom more than showing up because, by this time, the hauling business had become the primary reason for my existence.

Somewhere in my mind, I began to resent not being allowed to attend school even if I was uncomfortable within my skin, the classroom, and energetic work ethic and skills. For years I was grateful, I had attended school the day the assignment to draft a story was given. I am not sure how that happened. I very seldom attended school two days in a row. However, it could have been a Friday the teacher assigned the story task, and the following Monday to present. I had not developed a word bank. I was excited to stand in front of the classroom, a holy mess. When the time arrived, I held one sheet of notebook paper in my hands primarily to hide my shame. Standing before the class, I made up my story, pretending to read my Once Upon a Time Script. I had sat in the back of the truck, trying to think out a storyline. I was fascinated by the word *FRAGILE*, written seemingly on the hundreds of cardboard boxes torn and stacked inside the large trucks.

A process that went on for three hundred and sixty-five days a year for eleven years. I knew what the term *FRAGILE* implied on the one hand, but I was unfamiliar with how to connect the word to a storyline. When the teacher asked if anyone was ready to present their assignment, I raced to the front of the class at breakneck speed. I started reading fast and furious, fearing that the teacher would order me to return to my desk before allowing me to finish. Instead, I dashed back to my seat at the end of my free-flowing thoughts. I did not know I could feel so humiliated. I was hungry for approval from God, anybody, even myself. The entire classroom was eerily quiet for a long while.

Fast forward about five years later. My parents demanded that I enroll in the Arline Jefferson school of cosmetology. While they made the first payment, I began working outside of the home to pay my tuition. Eviction from their home came a year later. There was no verbal exchange, just a couple of two-by-four planks of wood nailed crisscross the entrance of my upstairs living quarters of the family home.

When I stepped out into the wild wide world of being an employee, my first struggle was to accept my reality. I was unprepared for life on all levels. The terms soft skills and hard skills were still in the making in the early 1960s. My work world gifts were ghastly noticeable to a fault by all concerned, even me.

I was spiritually hungry, physically exhausted, and emotionally hopeless. I feared people, places, and things; it had an overwhelming effect on my introduction to the real world. Finally, I opened my first and only salon in 1969. The next subsequent struggle that I noticed on a deep level was my complete lack of communication skills. It wasn't easy to have meaningful conversations with my clients.

By 1972, I walked away from the salon business and decided to study for my General Educational Degree, which I received in 1974. However, I continued to hold odd jobs while taking one secretarial training course after another. Last I counted, I had held thirty-two various positions. It was as if I would appease my hurt by obsessively hunting for a job, then frantically relieved to find one, only to quit. It became a vicious cycle of winning and losing or catching and releasing. Soon, maintaining employment became an additional struggle.

My struggles began when I realized I was short on life skills. Unfortunately, my progress seemed small and insignificant for a long time.

I had begun to drink socially in my late teens. Then, in my early twenties, I began to need to drink obsessively to feed my struggling unidentified thirst and hunger. While I had a poor appetite for food, *the thought of soft drinks* turned my stomach, so I developed a stronger desire for alcohol. A few years later, the obsession grew stronger and stronger. *Finally, in 1977, I checked into the world's most sought-after treatment center at thirty years of age.*

Restrained from alcohol for two months, I found a job as a counselor at a place called The Wise Council House. I held that position for only one month before discovering that I loved being sober but not coaching clients. Although the employer was petrified and screamed, "You will never hold a job!" I calmly said, "Yes, I will," and walked away. For a moment, I wondered what made me say "Yes!" to my fragile lifestyle. But as Martin Luther King, Jr. once said, "We can't stop there."

After being sober for twenty months, I noticed I had been employed with a manufacturing company for eighteen months without the urge to walk off, not one time. I began to feel it was safe to enlarge my healing territory. I resigned from that job in 1979 after I received a position at the Division of Family Services. I managed to maintain this position for six solid years. Looking back now, I was still in training, if only to repetitiously show up for work at the same job. Nevertheless, I was grateful to have solved the pattern of quitting jobs. I was sure it was still just temporary healing, but it proved to be long-term.

I resigned from the DFS and relocated to Seattle, Washington, in 1985, enrolling in a computer training course. Once I completed that course in 1986, I became an office assistant at the University of Washington, which lasted for twenty-two years.

In 2003, I received my BA degree—yet, I was still starving for something other than being sober and having a degree. I sensed I was suffering from stages of spiritual starvation. I realized I was spiritually dying for soul relaxation, which included self-approval, self-acceptance, self-confidence, self-compassion, and self-love. I wanted to hear the inner emotional words, "Good job." But, I kept dismissing this "good job" inner referendum need.

Finally, when I became a gambling fiend in 2004, I could no longer ignore the core value call of self-praise. Every preacher, motivational speaker, and life coach shouted from the mountains and rooftops that the great news was helping others. Helping others was a great solution until I noticed I was getting nowhere with my emotional and spiritual development. Perhaps, I was living the animated version of "talk is cheap." Living in my truth was initially complicated, nerve-racking, and just plain scary.

The people I was trying to help seemed to be making considerable progress with phrases like, "Fake it until you make it," "Act as if," "This too shall pass," and "Lean on me" for support. That's when I had to take the words, "We are self-supporting through our own contributions," and relate them to our aid toward emotional development.

I found medication vital in the first three months of my new non-gambling solution. After that, I hired a coach to stay focused on the new lessons of truth. My life became one large classroom. I became the teacher and the student simultaneously. I knew I had to face the fact that self-support, self-approval, self-acceptance, self-compassion, self-esteem, and self-love were all core values to be examined daily without becoming vain, arrogant, conceited, self-anointed, self-appointed, and right down petty. I had to investigate my mindsets daily. Along the way, from ineffective to practical, I finally found self-confidence. I stopped putting everyone else above me. I finally learned to live and let others live.

In 2010, freed from gambling, I was thankful, indebted to a power greater than myself. I no longer was bound by the things I could not change. Instead, I can change many things: my lifestyle, thinking, seeing, and actions; I can embrace many basic self-approval concepts.

To stay sane and balanced is to focus on what I am doing right, ask for help when I need help, keep an "I am good enough journal," improve upon self-confidence, watch my spoken words, find a coach if all else fails, and continue to be a worker among workers.

I know that the unfed healthy instincts and desires only grow hungrier if not fed. My hunger instincts are now only hungry to succeed. And, in the end, it wasn't just the words "Good job" that I craved; it was "Great job," and maybe someday "Excellent job," that I desired to embrace.

Sometimes I still ask myself how I got involved in sober living? I am not sure, but being sober for me helps me allow life to make more sense. Still, I grapple with connecting with a wide range of principle dots, trying to stay in the arena of rational thinking, doing, and living.

Disappointment soon became my platform for strength-building. I began to see, feel, and believe in divine power. I had reached another turning point. Today, I do not panic so easily; figuring out solutions has become a new and different lifestyle choice. A substantial degree of spiritual discovery finally made its way to the outstanding proficiency column of my "soul report card."

Great God that you are; thank you for allowing my many indicators, warnings, signs, wonders, footprints, dreams, clues, struggles, fits of hunger, and seemingly hopeless trials that became hints of a neglected soul. I finally concluded that I could not fix myself; I became tired of trying.

Write about spiritual pangs of hunger fulfilled in your life.

I was alarmed one day while I
stood afar looking at the bench of
hopelessness and encountered
a vision of hope.

3

The Spirit of Hope

A sector of GRACE

"It is such an honor to receive the gift of Hope."
—Anonymous

At the age of six, thinking back even before I started school in 1953, my hopeless little world, draped in colorless shades of gloom, beckoned my attention on several occasions. Making myself useful by climbing into the tall trucks was only the beginning of an eleven-year routine. My afternoon school program began with many hauling trips to and from the Country Club Plaza.

When I arrived at my first and last treatment center in 1977, I had been severely, dramatically, and repetitiously shamed. Drinking had been a warm and bitter cover for my emotional emptiness. It was a solution, or so I thought. Many disgusting, appalling, and horrifying occurrences had happened along the way; I later termed those behaviors as symptoms of untreated childhood trauma. It was a journey of obscure behaviors passed on from generation to generation. At last, I knew what did and didn't work for this sister. I learned that a person can be drinking or sober and still act irresponsibly.

First, I had to address my hopeless mental attire. Being evicted should have pushed me over the edge, but it pointed the way to better. I figured I could try to make myself proud once I had survived the childhood lifestyle. It had not been easy. In 1966, I married for the first time; three years later, I divorced for the first time. As I like to tell the story, he was a great guy; he was just not up for a broken-spirited person like me. I wanted to find a better me. After the divorce was final, that's when the relocating seemed to pick up in speed and need. I needed so much, and hope was one of the things I knew I needed pronto.

I looked for hope, mainly in clubs, churches, and relationships. But instead, what I found was a more profound sense of hopelessness within and around me. It seemed that people were okay with their hurt and pain. I, on the other hand, wanted my hurt, pain, shame, and all the rest of my brokenness to be removed—to be cleansed, white as snow, or at least a washing that would allow me to want to live within my skin and leave me feeling fresh and clean inside and out.

I wanted my burdens rolled away, not all of them, but some. I wanted to know the meaning of being born again; the unknowingness flooded my soul. But unfortunately, incompetence stood firm in the way of me finding solutions for my spiritually malnourished soul and body.

As my developmental processes continued, I simultaneously learned I could be happy and sober. I could put away childish behaviors. I could admit the truth, make decisions, and investigate my weaknesses and inadequacies. I could lose that feeling of being distant, lonely, and detached. I could come to believe in a spiritual way of life that I understood. I could live and let others live with ease and comfort. I could seek and find inner peace. I could live in this day. I could begin to want to accept the things I once could not shoulder. I could start to honor gratitude. I began comprehending the word "serenity," just like I finally came to believe in God. I began to understand the word "hope" before I knew its definition through vestige and envision, or before I felt HOPE!

I never had much use for the expression or ideology of "hope." As a result, my understanding of feeling hopeful was slow to come. I did not know that a bit of hope would lift my spirit and change my known state of impossibility to possibility. Going without a drink for a couple of days was nothing new for me, for I did not drink all day every day before I stopped drinking altogether. I wondered why I was so excited to accumulate a third day, a fourth day, a first month, a second month, one year, two years, and now forty-five years. I soon learned that is the pattern of a process. I did not intend to remain sober; it was like my hike with relocating. I did not plan to wake up the beast of musical chairs in my life. Instead, I looked up one day and I depended upon the relocating energy associated with appearing busy. First, it seems like a workable solution, then a sport, and then an unnecessary full-blown obsession.

Back to my story of anticipation and hope, it began to seem like there was a spirit of hope that would not leave me alone. Each day I would say to myself, *I wonder if I can stay sober one more day?* The more I contemplated being clean and sober, the more I wanted sobriety. I do believe this was the first time I had experienced gratefulness. I did not get too excited because I thought the new outlook on hope was only a one-day-at-a-time blessing or soon to be an I-told-you-so-curse. I did not know how to do life, but all the burdens did not take away my hope this time. I begin to wonder what happened. Usually, I became entangled in the mighty powers of the syndrome of struggling. Then I would lose my focus with an acute quickness, allowing my ever-ready spirit presence of panic and impossibility to take charge.

I learned that being accountable is an equal opportunity. So, when I walked into my first healing facility, I heard hope, saw hope, felt hope, and even knew it was hope before I knew I was hopeless. Somewhere along the way, my parents used to hire drunks to help in the family business. Somehow, I compared skid row bums to hopelessness and compared myself to the skid row bums. I have learned that a skid row mentality starts in mind. Forgiving my children and my parents allowed me to move to a deeper level of hope.

I found forgiveness for my parents. I was amazed at the toxic power unforgiveness brings. Not forgiving them allowed me to be the best parent even while measuring my parenting skills against theirs, which proved ineffective for the results I sought. When I could forgive myself for being an inadequate parent, I could correct my intensely aggressive, emotionally ruthless screaming at my two children. When all was said and done, I began to utilize the spirit of speaking lovingly to my children and others and desired to change my self-talk.

I knew then and today that when hatred within is all one has, they can only give that. So when I was ready; to make amends to my parents, children, myself, and anyone I intentionally or unintentionally damaged in my wake, I had to refashion my spirit of kindness.

Looking at my self-centered fears and many flaws allowed me to remove the residue of unforgiveness to forgive my parents and myself. My hope started to appear when I saw the value in not drinking. I noticed that my level of hope grew when I took the necessary actions. I saw a job-hopper change into a well-valued employee. I began to hear hope in words like abundance, faith, acceptance, release, belief, power greater than myself, trust, honesty, open-mindedness, and willingness. The literature I read pointed out how to change from hopeless to hopeful.

My initial burdens rolling away made room for life's up-to-date daily challenges. I could choose to release them and enjoy the freedom of them being gone. I did not have to struggle with situations because they had a possibly deceptive, seemingly vibrant energy, causing me to remain stuck longer than necessary, wearing me out.

Do you recall a time when you realized
you had acquired some semblance of HOPE?

By the time I realized I'd embarked upon
the bench of willingness, I was ready to
turn over my will, which had bullied,
coerced, and browbeaten me into
doing it my way far too long.

4

The Spirit of Willingness

A component of RENEWAL

"When I realized I needed to stop
trying to be somebody else and be myself
that I started to own, accept, and love what I had."
—TRACEE ELLIS ROSS

A component of self-renewal is a crucial part of the spirit of obtaining the willingness. Up until the age of thirty, I was bored to death. I could not figure out when or how I started to be so acutely bored with life. Finally, I concluded I had been bored for as long as I'd known myself. I was bored, depressed, and grieving, and I grew resentful. I was not keen on displaying relevant life skills. Covering up the boredom, the depression, and the grief was a full-time job.

If life got too dull, I would relocate not to feel the true boredom. Looking back at the eviction, it was a wake-up call. The displacement awakened me to a desire to create a healthier lifestyle for myself. However, the willingness was not there yet. I had to spend much time understanding why my parents could not see some value in me. What I learned finally came in the form of a question: Was it possible they did not know the value within themselves at that time? I was asking for the impossible.

Meditating on life's principles in a hopeless state of mind and body was challenging. It was impossible to be willing to examine my truths. Truth is a complex emotion to face. It took some years to let go of what was. But, little by little, I became willing to do the soul work required to let go of pointless pain.

I had to figure out what I wanted to do with my life. Being unwilling to turn my old life and will over to a power greater than myself had significant repercussions. Much of the aftermath had results I did not want to face. Yet, I was still without the strength to face many facts about my life. My truth was that I existed in a world of self-pity and loneliness, running from church to church, club to club, job to job, and problem to problem without a solution base.

Until I was willing to let go of my old unwilling baggage, I could not become ready to try different well-balanced experiences. I noticed I began to laugh more and complain less. I began to say "please" and "thank you" more readily morning, noon, and night. I was willing to network with others, research, study, read, and write more during my free time. Moments of quietness were a long time coming. I became a stranger who wanted to change my self-talk. I became someone I did not know.

I became tired of speaking to myself in fits of rage and wanting others to talk to me with admiration. I was drained of the aches of discontentments. I yearned to get the humor of a joke, laugh at a comment, or feel promised joy from the universe, but none came fast.

A lot of my willingness came from hindsight. I tried to resist and found it counterproductive to become happy, joyous, and carefree. People would say, "Enjoy the joy," and I wanted to say, "Tell me how and I will." In the beginning, the willingness to change was a process I cannot explain. But, I know today I am happy, joyous, and untroubled. One of the things I am most happy about is that the old me no longer rules my life. But, there is a time to face the truth and realize, recognize, and release the untruths. The spirit of rebuilding is refreshing.

Explain an act of will that changed your life for the greater good!

Part Two

Honoring the Spirit

(Celebrating)

The primary purpose of **The Spirit of Becoming**
*is to give more meaning to becoming
a whole human being, body, mind, and spirit.*

One day while sitting on the bench of past strongholds, my soul begins to release them one by one.

5

The Spirit of Letting GO

Shared praise of TRUSTWORTHINESS

Sometimes making a way out of no way is the miracle.
—LEONA P. JACKSON

My life did not have any meaning whatsoever. I did not know what to do, feel, or think. I had drifted off to sleep after the delivery at the hospital was over. Then, when I opened my eyes, a nurse holding a baby stood there. "Is that my baby?" I asked. The nurse replied, "Yes, but he's dead."

Once I was released from the hospital on the seventh day, I was unsure what to do or what I was supposed to feel. It was a relief not to have any emotions when I looked up and saw the nurse standing there with the baby in a slight sitting position in the cradle of her right arm. I drifted further into loss and loneliness, but I was at a loss for words. I was unfamiliar with the emotions of grief—it was difficult to face my sense of loneliness. I had not heard the word *suffering*, but that was how the family had lived every day for eighteen years. I did not know-how we lived had a name. It was called deprivation, existing, and survival. I returned to my upstairs room; and began listening to the late great Aretha Franklin on my small record player, singing, *God Will Take Care of You. When?* I wondered, over and over. *When is the God Aretha singing about going to take care of me?* I continually asked and re-asked. All I could do was sleep during the day and look out the window at night, thinking about the power of death. Listening to Aretha Franklin, by day and night singing, *God Will Take Care of You.* It had been my unconscious spirit-filled pastime since losing my baby and being dismissed from the family business. So, I was not only grieving the loss of my child but pushed out of the family business. My parent's ritual was to dismiss each child from the business on their sixteenth birthday.

I began doing everything I could to forget what had just happened. Once I was home, *I wondered if it was a policy to show a deceased baby to the mother. What was the point?* A few days later, I replaced the death experience with the visual provided by whoever had taken the liberty to nail two two-by-four planks of wood crisscross the entrance door of my upstairs room in the family home. I turned around and walked back down the eleven or so steps and began making mental choices to replace the recent occurrence of birth and death, neglect and abuse, and eviction and homelessness.

I found a duplex, a job, a husband, and had another child, trying to make life right again, at what I had called "life right before the loss;" that was a three-year process. I was unsure if there was such a thing as a spirit of life. As Whitney Houston used to sing, *How would I know?*

My life had always been drab and filled with sorrow. I continued to wander and wonder. Finally, a still, small voice ever so gently said,

"You have got to leave here." With that, I dismantled the entire show of my life and stumbled upon many different answers.

I started another job, sold my furniture, and began to walk off jobs without prior notice. At last, I decided to return to the beauty salon world. I was working in one shop when a salon owner approached me with the idea of establishing my own. My shop was finally in operation, but I no longer wanted to be a part of this new adventure and found I could not will myself to do so. The weight of my broken spirit was far too heavy. So, I relocated.

Trying to find God, the spirit of life, me, and some sanity was the order of the day. I picked up on the drinking and sadness as I moved from place to place. I was somewhat relieved that I always seemed to have the discernment to leave uncontrollable messes. *I now know that I had constant unstoppable mental debates in my mind about drinking and not drinking.*

Choosing to say goodbye to drinking has proven to be one of the greatest vital gifts I have ever given myself; with the traded gift came the spirit of love, happiness, peace, contentment, self-care, teamwork, willingness, greater self-control, management, and freedoms galore. In addition, the ability to let go of many things became conceivable—the spirit to work with others and a feeling of usefulness at last. Hitherto, a new outlook on life found me and immeasurable opportunities.

Much toxic baggage vanished when I took the actions needed to produce a flamed, enthusiastic, dynamic, and practical set of empowered coping skills. I now have self-control and self-confidence. Today, I can trust the God of my understanding unapologetically. Yet, I know there is so much more to come, pleasant and unpleasant. Gifts of the Spirit did not come overnight like express mail. Being wedged between knowledge and a lack of confidence is sometimes one of the most awkward transitional spaces. Something needed to happen to transfer from chaos to peace, but I was unsure what. I was not willing to step into the spiritual repair shop initially. I am still working on a mind-shift of greater self-love. I am finally beginning to respond more often to the humorous side of life. My life always seemed like an untold story, and I had difficulty making the many chapters. I had a complicated time following the untold storyline as I lived it. Writing the story finally became much more rewarding than living through the unscripted tale of woe. I finally learned to let go of the many things I can't change daily. Practicing letting go has caused me to become more trustworthy of my motives, intentions, and peace of mind.

What do you believe hinders you from letting go sooner than later?

*"Those who move forward with a Happy Spirit
will find that things always work out."*

—Gordon B. Hinckley

Somehow the bench of gratitude finds me daily.

6

The Spirit of Gratitude

A shared expansion of FREEDOM

Feeling sorry for myself was among my many emotional handicaps. I had to challenge plenty of unproductive habits before I genuinely developed an attitude of gratitude. I learned gratitude is not a statement but a feeling with unprecedented benefits.

I could not see, hear, or find anything for which to be grateful for a long time. However, I was genuinely thankful for my struggling sobriety from the beginning.

Once upon a time, my sobriety date was my only tangible core value. I would try to be grateful, but I just could not. I could only be grateful momentarily. These brief gratitude episodes left me without the fundamental process. After a while, people would say, "You are not grateful," as if gratitude was a value one could purchase online. At the time, I believed the brief spurts of gratitude were insignificant; however, I soon realized genuine gratitude is a process. Those fleeting moments soon developed into more in-depth periods of gratitude. I have since learned that embracing gratitude and self-pity is impossible. You constantly strive to possess one while dismissing the other; it is a simplistic individual choice. My simple "Please in the Morning" and "Thank you" at night was my new beginning of shifting an emotion that is hurting rather than helping me obtain higher energy for which to practice thankful behaviors daily.

Once I was having a rough time with serenity, peace, and life in general while I was sober. When I asked for help, the person snapped back, "Write a gratitude list," and kept on walking with much haste. I wanted to say I am grateful for all my life is, but that does not spell "GRATITUDE." That says there is more work to be done. If I am lonely, I need to become willing to work through the process of deescalating loneliness until some semblance of contentment appears or reappears. If filled with uncertainty, I would need to repair, rebuild, and revamp my reservoir of assurance, trust, and confidence. If I am unhappy, I must dismantle the unhappiness until some happy factors emerge.

My writing down gratitude lists got me sitting at casinos buying expensive thrills of winning and losing, at least at first. The casino was a place where I could discount sadness even when losing. The bells, whistles, noise, people in motion, and colorful lights flickered with many patterns. It made me recall my childhood, making myself useful by climbing up into the tall trucks, which was only the beginning of an eleven-year routine. The highly sensory environment had a rhythm, while characters and objects on the machines performed outlandish tricks. Ultimately, my gratitude became winning jackpots with large and small cherries lining up in various systematic rows on the machine monitors.

I learned that I had to let many things go, like the expectations of others. The lesson is to let non-productive things go as soon as the truth is somewhat visible. I've also learned that the thankfulness process is a powerful tool to transcend old patterns of negative feelings and emotions into positive natural works of functional art. Finally, I knew appreciation is not about winning and losing but being thankful for the moment.

By forgiving, we disentangle ourselves from the toxic entanglements we have experienced, protect our spirit, and re-create healthy relationships where we are no longer affected by another person's bad choices, or our own, so readily.

Today I am grateful to have let go of the need to hang on to past chaos. Letting go is a facet of being free to live in this day. Today, forgiving has increased my spirit of thanksgiving. A heart of gratitude is a productive principle of being free—body, mind, and soul. The essence of gratitude is a shared expansion of freedom. Today, my world bears witness to God's love for me: I now feel that I reflect His magnificent image, like a light on a hill! I understand what Desmond Tutu meant when he said, "Being different is not intended to separate or to alienate; we are different precisely to realize our need of one another." I now know my identity flows out of how I think, speak, and act, no matter how much I try to suppress my identity. I now know when I have stepped out of my unique environment and created a toxic space.

What spirit is driving your emotional life? Self-pity is not my driver today—thank God! Instead, multiple drivers stand ready to support my journey. Some of the gifts of the spirits are forgiveness, joy, love, peace, patience, kindness, goodness, faithfulness, gentleness, mercy, self-control, grace, wisdom, knowledge, healing, miracles, service, giving, encouragement, empowerment, hospitality, and gratitude.

Have you made a Gratitude list?

"You'll be calm the day you learn to
sit alone and doing nothing."
—Maxine Lagacé

It was most challenging to rest on
the bench of self-confidence.

7

The Spirit of Self-Confidence

A shared engine of COMMITMENT

*"One day, I noticed my worth no longer depended
upon the assumptions of them."*
—LEONA P. JACKSON

I became employed at the University of Washington in 1986 in Seattle,
Washington. I had taken many classes during my work hours. In 1998,
I enrolled in Evergreen State College in Tacoma, Washington. It was
a thirty-mile drive to school three nights a week. I love the long drives.
The Bridge program at Evergreen was just the entry-level of learning
I needed.

Professor Morris at the UW tutored me on my lunch breaks. I can
vaguely remember asking her for help. I was thankful she looked over
my many faults and saw my apparent needs. I wanted to explain how I
came of age without formal learning skills. Some of my missing skills
were: self-confidence, my inability to retain new information, correct

grammar, spelling, writing sentences with subjects and verbs, thinking, and interacting with others. Instead, she plowed right on through one English task after another. Had not Professor Morris tutored me for those six years, my BA degree would still be just a wish.

One day I noticed my self-worth no longer depended on "them." Watching others and picking myself apart was an entrenched habit for many years.

I examined my creative self-leadership skills to stay free from depending on others to take the lead in my life. I became willing to release their influence. I noticed that getting my clues on what to do next by observing them was over. I started to listen to *them* instead. Soon I was released from their spell. Finally, I learned who I was, established, who they were not, and clarified my growth goals as a student of life through observation, information, and action. Finally, I had to make an effort to define the right self-development strategies for myself with the utmost importance.

When I sometimes find fault in others, I notice it's the perfect time to critique myself, releasing the critics. As I learned to implement new skills, I noticed that those around me might have sometimes gotten bitter before getting better. On the other hand, I became better because of the opportunity for the learning experience I gained from watching them. Somewhere along the way, I became more and more a doer of truth, not just a hearer. I had begun to climb a plethora of learning mindsets of wealth.

While taking a speech class years ago, I found a recipe for gaining self-confidence in speaking. I was thrilled to have all the main ingredients for self-confidence on one little yellow index card: Yes, you can add other ingredients for flair, style, and smoothness.

The Ingredients of Self-Confidence

One pinch of Excitement

One dash of Anxiety

Two dashes of Certainty

One smidgen of Pride

Three dashes of Humor

One splash of Safety

Six tidbits of Fun

Four pinches of Presence

Plenty of Gratitude

Combine all ingredients, plan, prepare, and mix with love; know there aren't any quick fixes for presenting a bubbly speech to an eager audience. Rise gracefully, let your eyes steer, and stir the spirits in the room with each step. Smile when you are touched by observing signs of a connected audience. Be prepared to take your self-confidence off the stage with you, knowing you have incited, shifted, and stirred up the gifts in the crowd. Enjoy.

My mind is finally free to learn all I can about myself. One of the assignments of my mind is to catch the practical thoughts and build on them to construct a systematic healthy cluster of thoughtful, trusting, and core beliefs that hold much value for life and living. Gaining self-confidence is a process. Today, I love the feeling of being honest with myself. It's called *integrity*. I believe the spirit of self-confidence is a shared engine of commitment.

I am unsure what or when I crossed over from victim to victor.

Meandering around in the conquerors' sphere was a dreadful, uncontrollable, and sometimes toxic, stressful experience at first. I seemed out of place and, possibly, I was. It took some getting used to hanging around others and not knowing if it was safe or unsafe to speak from new and different levels of growth, non-growth, and new awarenesses.

I learned an enormous amount of knowledge from reading Brené Brown's books. I can hardly wait for her next book.

Who are the people in your life
which helps you rekindle your dwindling spirit?

*"Those that understand, SOMETIMES
no explanation is necessary and those that do not understand,
no explanation is SOMETIMES possible."*

—UNKNOWN

While driving with my seatbelt buckled tightly, I noticed a bench "marked" impatience, and then somehow, like a card reader, the word "patience" without the "I'm" flashed back and forth and became its replacement.

8

The Spirit of Patience

A shared fraction of RESILIENCE

*"The spirit of patience is sometimes caught
and sometimes taught."*

—Leona P. Jackson

There is a time to strive to become fully invested in healing and a time to release the conflict of being the recipient of a self-deceiving, self-serving, and self-annoying person. There is a time to make every effort to relinquish the unpleasant, dispirited, breathing self and a time to give way to owning new, natural fundamentals of happiness before and after breathtaking loving moments. Standing and being in a new and different self is one of the most significant rewards of patience. Who would dare to experience this great secret of having the spirit of tolerance and not owning it? Once you know the value of patience, you will not want to exchange it for impatience—the essence of patience is a shared fraction of resilience.

Learning to practice the art of relaxing, rearranging, and recharging one's spiritless routine to enrich one's life is vital. If you are an overly serious-minded person like me, learning not to take life too seriously all the time requires skill. Tolerance allows us to take a break from our mental impatience. Feeding our minds with wisdom, insight, and more understanding instead of being stuck in a permanent place of non-growth is exhausting. At the same time, patience is sometimes created by unlearning, deleting, and rejecting old, outdated, ineffective learned patterns of thought and actions when we become conscious of practicing new skills. Accepting or rejecting nonsense allows us to choose what growth fields to cultivate and eliminate while improving our self-guidance pathways.

This chapter, "The Spirit of Patience," is an opportunity to fix our internal and external chaos. It presents a platform designed for those who need to overhaul their reactions to the many healings of life. But unfortunately, creating patience talk is primarily for those who do not have the support, for whatever reason, from significant others, first-rate groups, successful daddies, educated moms, compassionate neighbors, or the coach of the year.

We are ordinary people who want to grow and develop with the most integrity possible.

Appropriate behaviors can enhance better networking experiences. Sayings have stood in the gap between instantly responding and feeling like a fool, serving as another coping mechanism when counting sheep, counting to ten, rehearsing the Serenity Prayer or the 23rd Psalm, or the like, aren't deemed effective in the moment. Sometimes I must listen to the whispers now to avoid the screams later. So, I created this exercise to calm moments of instant disturbance or buy some time instead of reacting hastily to an emotional situation. I have been guilty of acting in haste for many years. Today, I know it has a lot to do with my overactive amygdala gland. At the beginning of making personality changes, remembering all the facts, including what may be good about ourselves and others, can be stressful. You're not your best self when the amygdala is running the show.

Here are some things you can do: know your triggers, let go of the unproductive story, release the tension, and remember whom you aspire to become. I found that practicing these simple suggestions gives the mind a chance to regroup in an instant momentarily. We tend to believe that if it's popular, it's right. I heard someone say it's a chance to clear some space in the busy mind. However, the mind's primary focus is to think and chatter; if we are not careful, we will add too much emotion, energy, and attention to a thought that was only in passing.

Recovering from one addiction after another is not easy. This particular exercise would have served me well back when I was in the throes of my unwellness; just having wisdom seemed too easy, plus I believed that understanding wisdom was for saints. Just rehearsing the information (see below) in my mind would have prevented many unnecessary blunders had I been ready for such a mental mind task. There is a time to let go and hold on to yesterday's pain and misery— this is a national song of praise for victims. I used many prayers, meditations, what-ifs, and other repetitious methods during those unproductive times. Prayer and meditations do work. If you are a nonbeliever, as was I at the time, extra assignments would have given me something different to busy myself with while waiting for the many promised healings to show up. Patience is truly a virtue.

Patience is one of the twelve gifts of the spirit found in the Holy Bible. It is an authentic privilege to have some patience. Once upon a time, impatience ruled my life. Life is funny, with its rewards and timeouts. When I believed I had some patience to spare, my patience reserve showed up empty. The difference now is that I know this impatient moment will pass. There are days when patience is out of my reach, and I still struggle, but learning to pick myself up and get back in the race is rewarding.

Remember, there is always:
- A time to approve and a time to disapprove
- A time to shift and a time to drift
- A time to pack and a time to unpack
- A time to disagree and a time to compromise
- A time to fold and a time to hold
- A time to reap and a time to sow
- A time to plant and a time to reap
- A time to read and a time to write
- A time to question and a time to answer
- A time to increase and a time to decrease
- A time to listen and a time to speak
- A time to inhale and a time to exhale
- A time to give and a time to receive
- A time to pray and a time to meditate
- A time to seek and a time to find
- A time to teach and a time to learn
- A time to agree and a time to disagree
- A time to recognize and a time to ignore

- A time to value and a time to devalue
- A time to observe and a time to act
- A time to win and a time to lose
- A time to lead and a time to follow

What is "A time for you to *remember* daily?"

To be parked on the bench of certainty-is like no other when it comes to change.

9

The Spirit of Who I Am

An altruistic knowing of SELF-HONESTY

*Please do not stop telling us broken ones
our truth as you believe or see it!*
—Leona P. Jackson

The fulfilled law in a single decree in Galatians 5:14, "Love your neighbor as yourself." The whole fulfilled law is keeping this one command: "Love your neighbor as yourself." I believe loving my exterior neighbors is a direct commitment to valuing the neighbors within us as self-loving neighbors first. Then, and only then, one can genuinely aspire to love their external neighbors. But, finally, from within, I must hold the right to be authentically proud of who I am.

At the age of 25, while most young folks were checking out the latest dances, number one hits of the late sixties and early seventies, and fashions, visiting social clubs, capitalizing on establishing relationships, and playing single future heads of households, and so was I—I was also looking for courage soulfully. I briefly held the title of wife and then, long-term, single mother of two. My intense self-doubt made me believe I would never find any courage in a million years; the claws of cowardness wrapped me tightly. My lack of ambition somehow drove me to endure being locked in survival mode despite wanting to live one day. The spirit of who I am is an altruistic knowing of self-honesty. I somehow thought courage was the missing element. I did not know how courage invited itself into one's life, but I was willing to play hide and seek until I found out. I was bored and had much time on my hands to hunt. In the end, I found the courage and an innumerable number of principles I had no idea was missing. In the words of Maya Angelou, "Courage is the most important of all virtues because, without courage, you can't practice any other virtue consistently. You can practice any virtue erratically, but nothing consistently without courage."

When I checked myself into Western Mental Health one hot summer day in the early seventies, I realized finding courage required much more than existing in self-pity while waiting on an unexpected shift in life. Now, I know I was painfully tired of moping, lagging, and dragging around in fear, with my depression working overtime to keep my feelings absent from life and living. Nonetheless, I stepped up to the counter at the health center and pronounced my name. The phone call I had made moments earlier told them all they needed to know. The front desk clerk and nurses seemed to have been waiting for me. They asked a few more questions and fastened a plastic band on my wrist. After a while, I was given several pills and escorted to the fifth floor.

I started to faint inside the elevator; thank God a nurse was going up with me. I didn't sense I was looking for courage or anything else; I was tired. I had been tired since I was between four and five years old. By age six, my tiredness felt like a natural state of existence. My stationed mind was on self-doubt and non-bravery. The outlook, status, and a personal case study of my depression had been with me for far too long. Existing in survival mode was getting the best of me. The scrutiny was exhausting. I did not know that my type of feelings of detriment had a name: toxic. Thank God, it probably would have been a bit much for me to process.

Being accustomed to allowing the critics within me to govern my merciless mental challenges, I faced each moment of the day getting the best of me. It was my mode of operation. Thoughts of the many injustices floated through my wounded heart, body, mind, and soul. I felt bushwhacked by chaos, insecurity, and emptiness, like swimming in a sea of uncertainty and the heavyweight of being overly vulnerable. The mental beatings were plentiful, dreadful, and painful. I felt like I could not live believing I was: *a trash girl*. I thought I couldn't muster up the guts to change my trashy mindset. But I finally realized was I was a human being, God's child, and a female at best. And, I finally learned I could not think myself into a new and different way of living. I had to act myself into a new and different way of thinking. I had to have God's help to remove the seemingly immobile defects.

Now, I know change is a gift. I have since learned that not everyone's pain, shame, and ignorance cause them to search for change. People forget to tell us broken ones, "You did not get broken overnight." They fail to tell us broken ones, "Perhaps you were born that way—broken." They sometimes overlook telling us broken ones that it's a process of slowly moving from darkness to light, madness to glad, and spiritually dead to having spiritual awakenings. It seemed that confusion and chaos commingled like flashes of frightening lightning. They neglected to tell us broken ones that a unit staging masses of constructions within our body's, minds, and souls pyramid is in operation and *takes time*. The erratic behaviors, thoughts, and beliefs create insanity. Today, I know that where there is a will, there is a way, and there are millions of ways to heal, and not all of the ways begin with acceptance.

Some skillfully packaged brokenness lies within a plethora of toxic left-over residue. Painful experiences require time to connect the lucky, glad and promised dots. However, it was excruciating to begin the simple process of joining the plethora of sad, dull, miserable, unhappy, heartbroken, and blue dots. Still, I took the plunge and began to sort out the distressing dots, and my spirit began to change for the better. Admitting myself to the hospital was one of my sad dots, moving into position anonymously. I must say, I did not plan this course of action by myself. I believe the hospital's course of action was designed for me by a power greater than myself.

During my powerful hospital stay, what became apparent was that being conditioned to examine my pain, hurt, and discomfort had been my only reaction to life and living. Again, searching fervently for my praiseworthy strengths had been absent. There is a time to accept life on life's pitiful terms. (Ouch!)

After much rest and food, the group counselor at the hospital announced that we would circle up for a group meeting on the second day. There were maybe twenty or more of us. The therapist posed this question as she paced outside the circle: "Tell me, what would you do if you purchased a pair of shoes and, for whatever reason, you did not want them. Maybe they were the wrong color, too big, too small, too cheap, or too expensive; the heel was too high or low. What would you do?" Half of the clients spoke up, stating what they would do. I do not remember what the participants said before or after answering the question. I was preoccupied with anticipation, determination, and enormously edgy, trying not to forget my answer. My answer came to me as soon as the counselor completed the question. When my turn came, I spoke right up. "I would keep them," I said calmly and felt much relief. Although this was the first time I had shared within a group that mattered, I was exhausted and hurried to my room after the session ended. It was not easy to process what had just happened. I drifted off to sleep instantly.

After more rest and food on the third day, two therapists and I had a one-on-one session. My emotions overshadowed me. The session ended three to four minutes, or seconds, after it started. It was an overpowering moment if I ever had one. After more rest and food on the fourth day, I attended a group making a pair of moccasins. I thought we were a little off course with finding courage; nonetheless, I completed the tedious task.

Upon being discharged on day seven, I vowed never to tell a soul about the mental vacation. And, yet that was all I talked about to whoever would listen. I finally concluded that something was seriously wrong with my life; five years later, I checked myself into treatment. Perhaps my mind needed to be readjusted, recharged, or returned. I did not understand my behavior or why I was so serious about being born again. I just knew my unrest was my ruler. I know today that intentional thinking and actions are prerequisites for change. Emotions are not facts, misery is optional, thoughts are placeholders, and changing behaviors are the beginning of new life stories. The time came when I ultimately had to debunk my mental trickery to terminate the gnawing ache.

Today, I am a blissful woman who has self-forgiveness. I thrive on understanding the many plights of others and offer as much support as humanly possible without leaving myself back where I began my journey. I slowly became a "Yes, I can" person, with focus, intention, prayer, meditation, and many other great resources for ongoing team aids. I had built my personality from an abusive and emotionally unlit childhood. I wanted so badly to give what I did not have within.

I am a woman who has grown in self-love, self-respect, and self-forgiveness, unlike in the past when I found no reason to love, honor, or own myself. I now take pride in the person I am today. I am an empowered leader, a dedicated spiritual person who believes that hope always prevails as long as one lives. My belief in the human capacity to overcome odds and realize my dreams in life has been my cushion of comfort. This pillow of comfort has continuously moved me forward. I am a woman that has raised the bar for a higher level of confidence, discipline, and understanding.

I returned to school, received a BA degree, and added another cornerstone to my academic growth foundation. Obtaining a degree was like a time-out for me. It allowed me to develop more efficient self-care skills. As long as the encounter is within human capacity, I am a challenge seeker. Seemingly, being regurgitated from the belly of the beast, I am ready to live out the true purpose of my life. My desire to help others has allowed me to embrace becoming a potential motivational speaker, writer, and life skills coach someday, even if I am my only cheerleader, client, and candidate. I am also in the process of acquiring better financial management skills. I am grateful for my second financial coach. I have since learned about the importance of being my own best friend. I can now listen to what another person has to say actively and sort through toxic and non-toxic communication before the conversation is over. I am a person that practices the power of choice faithfully.

I want to thank whoever said, "I'm in the Whosoever Club." That's me. I do not wish to shut the door on the not-so-glamorous life of my youth. However, I have learned to value comprehending a life of serenity and peace, a worthy choice. I have released the early period of incomprehensible demoralization, which set my once unfavorable, earlier lifestyle in motion.

Whenever I offer a motivational speech, I focus on the importance of self-love, self-care, and self-control. Care, love, and control are three vital factors that have helped me overcome my fears, tears, and uncertainties and supported me in becoming the joyful self I am today. I like what Eric Thomas said: "When you want to succeed as bad as you want to breathe, you'll be successful."

A lot of my continual growth stems from the historical stories of others heard or seen in revamped their journeys for us to take notice of how they became renowned winners. For example, I finally listened to the words outside of my head that terrified me as a small child as I worked in the family sanitation business; in the movie *"On the Basis of Sex,"* asked by one of the judges in the film sarcastically, do you think women should be sanitation workers?

What does let the spirit have its way mean to you?

Part Three

Maintaining the Spirit

(Daily)

*Sitting on benches of encouragement is a spiritual
dress rehearsal of reading, growing, and thinking.
The soundness of mind is the takeaway—*

I've noticed that swinging my legs while benched sometimes warms my heart.

10

The Spirit of Self-Control

An altruistic knowing of
WHOLEHEARTEDNESS

"All I knew was the running, the chasing, and ranting
was over, and I still could not let go of the self-defeating
thoughts, fix the self-centered issues, nor understand
my plethora of problems. I believe it's called surrender."
—LEONA P. JACKSON

On March 4, 1977, I arrived in Kansas City, Missouri, from Lubbock, Texas. I can't remember if it was by bus, plane or train. My last tossed back and forth stop finally happened. Scripture tells us: *We henceforth be no more children, tossed to and fro, and carried about with every wind of doctrine, by the sleight of men, and cunning craftiness, whereby they lie in wait to deceive.* (Ephesians 4:14 NKJV) It was not the wind of doctrine nor the sleight of men. It was in my mind that mass production of cunning craftiness laid in wait to fool me thousands of times. The ability to get tired of the self-betrayal, cunning, baffling, and powerful tricks of my mind

65

repeatedly played on me, often began to seem natural, dangerous, and frightening.

A feeling of now-or-never knowing attacked me again. The surfaced feeling was not in a deep or lengthy segment, it was wispy, flimsy, and fleeting, but I sensed its intent. I had to choose what seemed like the thousandth time to live my life better. I had to choose to behave differently. I had to be willing to trust in this unseen power greater than myself—unknowingly. My soul seemed doused in hopelessness.

Seemingly, I could not afford not to trust this time. My tattered mindset quickly questioned why self-control was so difficult for me. *Why was it so grueling to want, desire, display, come by, or even possess principles, purpose, or connectedness? But,* I asked myself what *I had to lose, nothing?* Scripture says, "He restoreth my soul" (Psalm 23:3 KJV). I had experienced this now-or-never, emotionally wishing, sprint spirit. There was no believable sign of hope or desire within me that suggested a possible miracle was mildly possibly in the making.

My normal suspicious feelings vanished for a quick second. I was not sure if it was possible to settle down and provide roots in one place at a time. Nonetheless, I was somehow up for the challenge. I somehow perceived it as possible, even if it was only in my subconscious domain.

In the first years of my adult life, I had lived at twenty-five or so residences before choosing to leave Kansas City, Missouri. Still, I became aware that I was not too fond of Kansas City, Kansas, Albuquerque, New Mexico, Lubbock, Texas, or even myself, for that matter. So this time, I stayed put in Kansas City, Missouri, for eight long, numb, and chaotic sober years. At that time, I deemed *sober* as the defining word.

When I arrived in Kansas City that day, I had stopped by the home of one of my siblings. I walked around the back of the house to peek at their basement. Finding instant temporary shelter for my family was the plan. I wanted a place to figure out my life. Gifted at creating spur-of-the-moment choices was an element of survival living. I was unsure if I could become less sporadic, erratic, or chaotic. My mind was foreign to any degree of self-control, self-discipline, or self-reliance.

I sat on the top stair step of their outdoor basement entrance. As I sat with the hot sun beaming on my back, looking out over the entire view of the basement, all I could see was mud, mud, and more mud; in place of the walls and the floor. The builder had not taken the time to complete the basement's interior for some reason.

The circumstances that drove me back to Kansas City did not prepare me for the bizarre view I now sat facing. When I collected myself from the sight, the intensely hot sun, and the mud, I shook my head in disbelief and cried out, "God, help Me!" I am unsure where the rest of the discombobulated day carried me in such an emotional, oppressive, foxes-have-holes tragic moment. It's amazing how we remember such precise seconds of defeat and nothing else before or after those seconds in time. I knew beyond a shadow of a doubt that the basement view was not a choice. However, the muddy scene reminded me of the totality of my life at that moment. My recollection of the solution I made for shelter does not serve me now. A life without hope was and is a scary place to ponder – my nerves were raw, and the humidity seemed stale, clammy, and dreary. I was perplexed. As I sat gazing across the scenery of the basement view for what seemed like a long while, I could not imagine what I would do. I could not accept that this was my life, a mud-fest. I felt lost, afraid, and more vulnerable. For a brief moment, my emotions were without control. It was difficult to contemplate how I felt moment to moment most of the time.

It was one day at a time during those eight years in Kansas City, Missouri. I could stay sober, be stable, and have some self-control. However, the mud-spattering experiences made the outcome of my life foreseeable if I did not change my lifestyle. Combining hindsight, insight, and foresight creates a convincing shift in one's thinking ability. It was 1984 when I moved from Kansas City to Seattle, Washington, and continued to pursue my personal and professional goals.

Today, I have a new attitude and outlook on life. My mind is open to a new understanding of living thy worry-free lifestyle. I figured I could hold on to my sanity by day and night if I remained willing, ready, and prepared to have new experiences. I learned to create a sane, healthy, and reasonable way of thinking and believing. I now practice being responsible for the energy of my thoughts, actions, and outcomes I display.

How do you raise your spirit when you fall victim to a low mood?

"AS I developed a definition of wealth, my spirit coached me to investigate and unlock a stored treasure of self-honesty, research, and practical steps, making the wealth struggle plausible, digestible, and achievable."

Being benched sometimes has undesirable or welcoming effects; you choose!

11

The Spirit of Wealth

An altruistic knowing of ENTHUSIASM

> *"Wealth is the product of man's capacity to think."*
>
> —ALEXANDER POPE

It was 1965, and I was seventeen, when I saw my natural reckless handling of money and my lifestyle of poverty up close. It was my first job outside of the home. I had always withdrawn from my paycheck before payday every two weeks the entire year I was employed. So, when payday arrived, my check was nothing. But I had many other hurdles ahead in managing my money. So, I chose not to worry about the mismanagement of my funds, at least not then.

With my first job, I reckoned with the complex reality of my lack of insight into financial matters. I assumed I would grow out of the spellbound variations of the spending obsession at that young age. Instead, I went through a pawning and re-pawning progression over thirty years. The spending methods became different, but the results were always the same: I was penniless. I could make little sense of any gambling cycles that had gripped my out-of-control mind, body, and spirit from 2004 to 2010. While listening to the many earsplitting musical arrangements, colorful bells and whistles created by slot machines were maddening; unbelievable distractions drove me insane as I sat watching and pressing buttons while listening to the crescendo of music while being robbed of my dollars, cents, and sense. I could not control my impulsive thoughts as they rationalized the need to win more jackpots while, in reality, I was losing. I could not contain the mixture of outer conflicts, inner struggles, the underprivileged behaviors, emotions, and a surplus of instincts of a wretch undone.

Today, I know firsthand just what makes a menace to society. I could not sleep, nor did I have an appetite for food, and I had no power to think any non-toxic thoughts. At first, my uncompromising thoughts seemed irrelevant, unrelated, and separate from my shipwrecked financial reality. I was bent on finding the original comfort of gambling that I once had felt, but I never did; I had to surrender to that fact. It was an uneasy, confusing, and chaotic paddle back to the shores of non-gambling thoughts. The spirit I felt was beyond any rational sense. I even tried to make peace with my farfetched loss of control.

My pathological journey sent me through miles of compulsive impulsivity and highly overwhelming, uncontrollable spending attacks. Compulsive gambling is repulsive, and the excessive appetite happens so swiftly that it is impossible to grasp its deep dimension of complexity, intensity, and intentional financial ruin. It was almost as if the objective was to see how fast l could get rid of any money I received.

There were no more paper payroll checks; it was the time of automatic deposits. It was no more disappearing to the bank on my lunch breaks. Instead, I spent the next fifty-six-plus years like a person with addiction written on every breath I took. I went through many phases; the shock phase, the numbness phase, the guilty phase, the emotional phase, and the painful memories of the many failed attempts to do better.

I spent excessive time in denial about my unstoppable financial madness. I was trying to control it, but I could not fix it. So, I spent even more time looking for easier, softer ways to amend my vicious spending behaviors. But unfortunately, it seemed as if the more I tried to control my unsuccessful financial behavior, the more I sped farther into a cesspool of economic devastation, panic, and emotional ruin.

As I moved through the numbness phase without my permission, I realized that denial, resistance, and isolation had me traumatized. These states of mind became my guarded buffers against the overwhelming realization of my financial situation. I was grieving what I never had—self-control, what I had lost—a child, and the yesterdays that I could not let go of after trying for five-plus decades. Writing my first book, *Release Me*, gave me a time-out.

It is one thing to feel like a failure and another to be a failure and feel pathetic about it. As a single mother of two, I felt horrible about my initial inability to remain employed, guilty about my lack of money management skills, and not creating adequate funds to sustain my household. Yet, scripture tells us that those who mourn shall be comforted. I have lived to see the truth in this scripture in my own life. The old, uncomfortable disorders of my financial difficulties have passed.

I seemed plagued with more in-depth underlying addictions causing each healing process to be more chaotic and slower. So, I began to plead to God, working with coaches and counselors, taking class after class, and joining groups to straighten myself and my finances. In the beginning, I believed these stumbling blocks were habits, but as I began to recover from one after another, they were groveling addictions trying to take me out, as addictions do.

I heard one preacher say my truth while sitting at my computer, listening and typing. What stopped me was when he said he could make money once upon a time, but he could not manage it." It reminded me of Ecclesiastes 3:1-8, which talks about a time to sow and reap. So, I added that there is a time to make money and a time to manage money. Not too long ago, I held seven jobs, giving me at least thirteen paydays marked on the calendar. I was still living from paycheck to paycheck, but I was also spending like a wild, mad person through sound and fury. However, I was able to pay off many more debts.

I also signed up for an online course called "Course from Scratch" for a large amount of money which was a lot and a loss for a woman with unhealthy and unwise financial habits. I could not grasp the content, context, or curriculum process. I took another course three times without seeing any beneficial promise, so I thought until taking it a third time.

I've lost a substantial amount of money searching for wealth and success. Mismanaging money is one habit I have perfected. As I wrote my first book, the economic value was the farthest thing from my mind. At the end of each year's toil and sweat, I had nothing to show for my ongoing emotional, economic, or financial loss or gain. I am still in search of higher spiritual grounds. I published the book in 2018.

As I write what I hope to become my second book, I ask myself, where are the pressed-down-shaken-together-and running-over fears I once possessed? The abnormal worries are gone. I do not know when or how I became so profoundly impacted by anxiety; on the same note, I did not learn step-by-step how I became free from my abnormal fears. Yet, I am free to be the released version of me, and DEBT-FREE.

Are you messy with money? For many years, I was. After working diligently in the family business for eleven years, I was, among other deficiencies, financially illiterate. I have spent the better part of my adult life trying to understand and satisfy that resentment of not being good enough to be paid for my work as a child. My negative feelings about money were compounded and blended with the inability to love my family or myself. Financial management is still a wish in progress. But, to put it mildly, I know I am a complicated person by nature.

As I conquered my financial inadequacies, one at a time, I slowly became aware of how entangled my thinking about money, and its value was. I craved having money to spend for many years, much like one might crave chocolate, alcohol, or cigarettes—the craving for spending far outweighed the urge or need for a sound financial plan. As a result, it was very challenging to stay the course in developing financial tools.

I slowly realized I needed to educate myself on the vast evolving strategies related to the advantages and disadvantages of financial management, lest one would believe I had graduated from the class "Windy and Wild Spending." But, today, I understand better the reality of my finances and how emotional and physical management work together.

I can see how easy it is to continue the mismanagement of living from paycheck to paycheck. A sense of egotistical shame constantly hounded me between paydays. One day, I committed to building a functional financial life for myself. As I accepted the spirit of economic study as a discipline, I discovered I needed to be more aware of numerous factors impacting my approach to handling my money more productively.

The knowledge of financial life cycles was foreign to me. The natural influences of having an economic belief system were nonexistent. The desire to maintain a baseline financial attitude was absent. The importance of understanding wealth patterns was vacant. I was in pursuit of finding economic principles, one being financial confidence. I started to sharpen my financial intuition by doing more research. My financial strength and faith became a greater force.

The power of self-forgiveness began to make more sense. The luxury of saving, budgeting, and planning began to work as part of my financial foundation. The skills of strategic thinking and operating in the profound ownership of my economic change became real.

Before this realization, my effective internal financial team and my ineffective financial team were constantly struggling. Finally, after starting my first paying job at seventeen, I began having consistent deliberations concerning money. About 35 jobs later, the internal message became, *you have got to find a way to stop the mental and physical merciless, notorious financial behavior.*

My constant, disquieting, vexed spirit from my numerous payday loans, gambling sprees, pawning, and monthly bills, pestered me on paydays and between paydays for many years. Finally, the nutshell of my conning, baffling, and toxic excuses seemed to push me further and further into the depths of one failed attempt after another and spiraling toward financial ruin. My economic blindness, pain, strain, and drain would one day financially rob me of a decent future.

I could not get on track with my financial wealth-building goals for over seven decades. I understand the saying, "If it is to be, it is clearly up to me." Today, I must utilize, strategize, and organize my financial management tools and intentions. All I have seen and experienced, healthy and unhealthy, has led me to walk on a pathway of financial wealth building.

I believed that having a ton of money immediately at hand would solve the money mayhem, relieving the financial burden instantly. However, while that may be an answer, it was only an idea among many other failed attempts to think my way out of one toxic setup after another. All thought and no action continued to rob me of a sure-fire plan. Using auto-stash investing of small amounts of cash regularly and consistently served as a helpful essential step. It was a way of reinforcing an excellent wealth-building habit, one habit at a time. It also allowed me to practice the power of another wealth-building habit—"commitment building"—while harnessing the powers of technology. I noticed I was no longer competing with an impossible dream. I moved from the driver's seat and allowed someone else to steer the finance vehicle. I call it God power in the form of mentors who manage their money with a sense of ease and comfort, doing such things as paying extra mortgage payments or paying off their credit cards, vehicles, and loans.

The one area I chose not to stumble in anymore was my ability to become financially successful in supervising my economic method of life. Until I released enough poor financial mismanagement behaviors, my confidence toward obtaining better financial wealth habits remained out of control. I could not imagine myself with my finances under control. I had spent a lot of money and time but had not found any order to my financial outcome. Facing facts is a powerful and empowering part of the process of change.

The emotional side of financial stumbling has significantly subsided, thank God. First, it was most challenging to stop cheating myself in unethical customs. Then, one day, I could no longer view my finances as a meaningless task. By this time, I had found peace and understanding in the more significant areas of my life-changing processes. The essential areas of my daily life are my lifestyle, work ethic, personal development, financial gain, health, family, and relationships. Of the seven regions, only one falls short of the desired wealth improvement status.

As I wrote my definition of wealth, something seemed to unlock a treasure of more self-honesty, which made the struggle I have been in since 1964 detach itself from a solution. Learning about the fruits of wealth has made the financial climb well worth the work. Finding a financial coach was my core definition of wealth. The larger my income, the more messy, calm, detached, and blameworthy I grew. However, between monetary and material wealth thoughts, it became an invisible classroom. I am the instructor and the student. I became my instructor by being willing to create and research answers.

I once read an article that said most people with a "poor wealth mindset' don't realize they have it. That was not the case for me. I *knew*. It would not seem right tomorrow if I had any funds to show I was a worthy steward of a wealth-building system. My ability to think, plan, budget, or invest my finances with moderation yesterday seemed sinful. Beneath my antithesis of a wealth mindset, I knew I had to set goals, be patient, persevere, and maintain a wealthier attitude. But I was consciously and unconsciously reluctant to put forth the effort to support a wealth change. But when I would glance at my ability and inability to implement these things, it was so uncomfortable, complicated, and eerie to disown the sights of the ongoing financial unrest. The disorder was in every area of my life, so I found one little corner at that time in 1977 to correct until I could embrace the thought of being able one day to love a wealthier me.

Once, I thought I had arrived when I began winning dozens of jackpots at several local casinos around town. I wanted to find healthier financial tools, economic belief systems, and financial order. Unfortunately, it took me seven years to retract my mind, body, and soul, which had gotten lost in the whirlwind of chasing money, jobs, space, perfection, and running from myself. Furthermore, only God knows what else I was obsessively hiding, withholding, and denying from within. While winning and losing jackpots at the casino, the financial dismay, discomfort, and dysfunction quadrupled. The mental insight of gaining independent economic hope was thinner than I could have imagined and headed toward worse.

I mastered enough self-discipline to make contributions to personal money savings accounts. Besides, I can now see, feel, and believe that financial health, wealth, and well-being are possible. Plus, I am learning how to spend in moderation. However, I am still learning to shop with a list and a plan.

You may be wondering at this point why wealth is essential.

Having a clear "Why" keeps wealthy-conscious people motivated to achieve their dreams and watch their plans, passions, and goals, develop, evolve, and manifest timely abundance.

Wealth means letting the hero within taking the lead through influence, power, and solidarity. Wealth has a surge of force-feeding opportunities through exceptional time management and organizational skills. Wealth can change what is not working sooner rather than later when guided by effective habits, behaviors, and mindsets consistently steadfast in their influential roles.

So, what is wealth? It has a primary purpose while being focus-driven and can move forward with or without cheerleaders within arm's length and in harm's way. Wealthy people surround themselves with wise counsel, even if that wise counsel is themselves at times. A large number of rich minds are hungry for knowledge and understanding. Besides having a great deal of contentment, they know exactly where their money is going and what their money is doing, or not doing, for that matter. They are in complete control of their lives. Wealth is finding new opportunities to grow and develop long natural and spiritual lines to uplift someone else's day or perhaps even your own.

Changing my mindset has been huge in my growth and development on multiple levels. To alter my attitude or behavior has been difficult. It has been time-consuming and baffling. For example, I knew what was being trespassed against me, but I did not know how to fix it. Many areas of my life, mainly my finances, year in and year out, stayed out of control and unmanageable. Most of the time, I could not precisely define which part of my financial thinking and actions was not congruent with my desire to change. The twist between financially successful and financially unsuccessful behaviors was foggy. My financial struggle was from 1964 to 2020 on various levels. Was the answer simple, or was it complicated? Was it a huge problem, or was it something small? I finally decided it was my lack of self-discipline in all areas.

By the time I completed the three Financial Peace University classes, I had realized I was following the principles outlined without a great deal of effort all along. The process made a different kind of sense. Not having money was an okay mentality. It was tremendously challenging to imagine having a thousand-dollar emergency fund just sitting somewhere for a rainy day, as was taught in the first nine-week class. So instead, I would contemplate what I could nickel and dime the fund away not once but three or four times.

Fishnet stockings and ruby red lipstick were two of my favorite, repeated shopping impulses back in the day. The principles of the second class seemed not as distantly achievable, with the possibility that it could happen. I could save one thousand dollars overnight, but I could not leave it untouched for any substantial amount of time. I kept saving a thousand dollars, more than half a dozen, before I could—or should I say, was—willing to leave it alone and make it an absolute emergency fund and not an instant spending resource. Still, leaving that amount of money alone was too much, and I never seriously gave it a go. What it did do was stretch open my closed wealth mindset. I finally had to learn more about my "Why" about economic prosperity building. Once I broadened my baseline, the defeat of financial management's difficulties slipped away. My ability to see wealth and happiness being a productive part of my lifestyle stayed close. Accepting the thousand-dollar emergency fund idea gave me a sense of financial hope.

It reminds me of when I was a co-participant in starting a book club in 2015. By 2017, I could not see the group's hope soaring into a club of energy. It was the last straw when I wanted the group to research the topic of "Seven Streams of Income." No one was interested but my daughter and myself. I have since learned that sometimes the message is not for others. And, I have finally realized that it does not matter if you are maneuvering the desired ship solo when you are focused on your evolving processes soaring.

We are always manifesting each thought one way or another. As a result, we have informed energy and uninformed energy. Our informed energy manifests from our experiences and causes our thoughts and energy to create our successful financial reality in time.

My wealth definition is a worthy, peaceful, and robust operation that bleeds, blends, and saturates the life management skills that feed one until their training becomes a living story of success that reads: "Wealth building the honorable way." Wealth also denotes the willingness to forge purpose and competence. In addition, wealth building is an opportunity to share knowledge and learning service applications with others. It's a brand of the multiplicity family and the "say goodbye to the long-lived dearth" clan.

Wealth is an assortment not limited to but includes immeasurable liberties, attributes, elements, choices, focus, resistance, resilience, purpose, meaning, self-sufficiency, passion, mindfulness, leadership-presence, authenticity, control, and effective relationships. In addition, wealth entails freedom, aptitude, self-awareness, spirituality, happiness, empathy, focus, direction, time management, influence, connection, genuine self-control, commitment, a deep sense of certainty, education, a plethora of open-mindedness, awakenings, financial surplus, flexibility, and a host of other truth characteristics twisted, covered, blended, and weaved into one's enthusiasm. Finally, landing with financial serenity is an achievement best exemplified in this quote:

"Those that understand, no explanation is necessary; and those that do not understand, no explanation is possible!"

Can I honestly ask myself, am I unknowingly still blindly stuck within my toxic shame, or is the change needed not familiar to me because I have practiced certain unacceptable behaviors for far too long? Such as uncontrollable financial dysfunction. By authoring this book, my two-fold hope is 1) to see the financial rainstorm is gone and 2) to see a wealthier shift in my economic status. I have been seeking better economic changes for a long, long time. I have been a student of Financial Peace University three different times, intentionally. Primarily, I could see some financial hope, even in a small but noticeable way, after attending the course for the first time. When I first joined the class, I knew it would take at least three or more nine-week courses to shift my financially lazy mind to a financially energized mind shift, so it did. As a result, I am today finally physically and mentally economically literate. Being financially literate is one of the gifts of having a healthier spiritual awakening.

As Kahlil Gibran has said, "Enthusiasm is a volcano on whose top never grows the grass of hesitation."

Now debt-free, I have enrolled in the Financial Coach class not to teach others primarily but to extend my financial focus, uplift my spirit of wealth, and remain a lifelong learner in money management.

How do you know you have a mindset of choice?

It takes humility to sit upon
various benches of surrender!

12

The Spirit of Forgiveness

An altruistic knowing of EMPATHY

"Those who are made well are graced with the highest gift
of coming to the aid of those who are sick."
—JAMES CHRISTOPHER CONE

When I first considered leaving my journey of mental hell, after not looking in the mirror for many years, with both eyes open, it was a harrowing experience. I would open one eye quickly as I washed my face or painted on my makeup on a good day. Most days, I would avoid looking at myself in the mirror altogether.

I wish I could describe the struggle it took to not look at myself by 1977 and all of the years that paved the way to that year. It wasn't easy to process life on life's terms. I was stuck on holding others responsible for my mental freedom. I did not know the problem; I told myself I was too young to understand. Then life began, and I was no longer a young person but in a state of pure defiance; again, I wondered what the problem could be. I left home as a teenager knowing what I did not know but believed I knew. Somehow, to be insignificant was how I was taught, not so much in words as from hostile actions and conflicting messages from attitudes of indifference from myself and my parents.

Soon, ten more years passed, and I knew I had progressed to a level unknown to me. I had never been there, so I thought, but I recognized some of the mandates from other trials. I was now thirty years of age, and I sensed I needed to give up the witch hunt to find the road less traveled from the direction I was traveling. So I paused at the next intersection, wandering up and down, back and forth. Thus I began weathering the paths of impulsivity, compulsive, and soon self-proclaimed mental illness.

In reality, your camouflaged stories and my hidden stories ultimately disclose many miracles of power produced in time only by the Holy Spirit. I do not claim to be familiar with much knowledge about the Holy Spirit, but I know at most times, the Holy Spirit has been my protector and my defense for longer than I understood spirit presence. I believe that down through the years, the Holy Spirit's name could be "Time." Time seems to heal as one works through many regrets, doubts, and renewal processes.

I can vividly remember struggling through each self-improvement phase; each stage had its ticket to hell and back before willingness became the emotional reward of restoration.

One of my earlier lessons was that one rotten apple spoils the whole bunch. For me, some rotten apples were alcohol, gambling, and fear. Reluctantly, with my round fifteen mental fight with that life, I called out, "I give up!" to whom I did not know. I held on to my defiant ways and all the other toxic fears and troubles to the end while sitting in fellowship circles of healing. Introduced to new principles, phrases, words, and concepts of many new and different terms that promised me growth and understanding felt rewarding. Three of those words were honesty, open-mindedness, and willingness.

I readily embraced honesty and open-mindedness with each new day of restoration. The willingness allowed me to see and feel the effects of its power and then ease away from my mental embrace once I took a bird's eye glimpse. For example, once, I was in a relationship, and it was not your "Leave It to Beaver" type that June Cleaver had with Ward, her husband. This relationship was in trouble from the very start. Yet, I believed that all the energy it brought was worth the stress and mess I was falsely charmed by each hectic day. Several times, a quiet thought kept beckoning me to surrender and walk away. And, yet there was this surge of energy that insisted that I should stay with it and win the sickening battle of prolonged defeat. Long story short, I finally walked away without the willingness being in my favor.

I learned that day that some decisions are made upfront without the spirit of willingness. Of course, being willing makes the transition much easier after a while. But, where or how does one become willing to let go? Sometimes our entire being is filled with a plethora of timidity, unwillingness, and indecisiveness. I remember when the spirit of doubt and hesitation were my constant companions. Finally, however, there came a time when I had to let go of many unproductive partners.

A sense of willingness became one of my new partners. How does the potter say to the master, "Be thou changed," and the master obey the servant? I secretly wondered if the spirit of being "unwilling" would ease up. Today, I think the nature of unwillingness is a gift, and the spirit of willingness is also a gift; it's just that the benefits are different. I have had my time with both. The activation of power is in the choice.

The spirit of forgiving is within you; it is a part of the electrifying family. Be grateful for the progress made but continue developing plans to accept the things that cannot be changed and become willing to continue moving towards a more superior personal and professional improvement. I believe self-care is a form of releasing judgment, not just of others but of self.

At breakneck speed, ripping and nearly running back and forth to the "At The Moment" machine—better known as the ATM—at the casinos, it soon became a sport, an annoying nuisance, and then a deep resentment. To solve feeling offended, insulted, and outraged, I, "Ms. Addiction," set a seven hundred dollar starting fee for myself. Sometimes I would win two or three thousand dollars, more or less, give it right back, and leave the casino with zero dollars. But, for a while, it was always seven hundred or more. Once I left my debit card at home with a convicted feeling that I would go home if I lost my startup fee; after all, whatever I started with was indeed enough to lose and be done. Well, the unimaginable happened that night, and it was not even ten o'clock when I lost not only my startup money but my car keys, too. What did I do? I took a cab from Tacoma, Washington, to Renton, Washington—a fifty-two-mile round trip. I had another set of keys at home. When I returned an hour later with my precious debit card in the same cab, I never checked with the casino's Lost and Found to see if someone had turned in my keys.

I had stayed clear of the casinos for at least fifty years before my collision with the compulsion attacked. I suspected I was an at-risk, probable addictive gambler somewhere deep within. I didn't know there were names for the various types: professional, antisocial, personality, casual, social, action, and escape. And I didn't realize there were four types of compulsive gamblers: Type 1, Type II, Type III, and Type IV, ranging from, long story short, two or three months of fun straight to addiction.

I trudged through all six phases of the gambling addiction before I became willing to stop gambling. The winning, denial, stress, exhaustion, critical, rebuilding, and recovery phases; I can vividly remember struggling through each stage; each step had its trip to hell and back. Again, the quote is applicable here: *For those who understand, no explanation is necessary, and for those who do not understand, no reasoning is possible.* Today I highly respect those exquisite, innocent "At the Moment" machines (ATM). I'm talking about unconditional regard. The same is valid for drinking.

I found self-forgiveness to be one of the more complex choices to make in the line of forgiveness. Although it took a while to become willing to forgive some, overlooking self-forgiveness became intentional. The thought of self-forgiveness seemed inhumane for a long time: a horrendous, painful, and disquieting period.

Thank God for my first advisor, she was a living example of, *Though they slay me, yet will I trust thee.* She was a wholehearted being. Among her many attributes were soulfully laughy, bursting with integrity, highly inspiring, and exceptionally motivating.

Learning how to forgive and love self has been one of the most challenging assignments during the entire process of change. I believe forgiving myself was difficult because my self-worth seemed elevated in one sense but not enough to process self-forgiveness. Low and behold, when I admitted to God, myself, and another human being who I was, forgiveness began to feel obtainable. I could not immediately forgive, but the possibility of self-forgiveness was deemed more conceivable.

Self-forgiveness brings on a greater sense of ease and comfort, more often than not. One can consults systems and strategies striving for bigger dreams, using more kind words, saying, "I love you," allowing others to offer words of kindness, appreciation, and praise. I can laugh silently or aloud, smile, be silly, share, say "please" and "thank you," be authentically grateful, keep my promises, help others, and stop and stay whine-free about what was wrong. I can see what's ethical and well with my soul, take more tea breaks, try new things, keep calm amid the storms, and carry on with or without an emotional blueprint. For me, the spirit of self–forgiveness is a shared altruistic knowing of empathy.

At this phase of my development, life is not a battle to be fought each day tirelessly. Life is to be lived in good spirits unless an experience dictates otherwise for a spell. My feelings now know a new freedom and new happiness. Self-approval feels at an all-time high; serenity, satisfaction, and happiness are regular daily companions. Depression, insensitivity, self-pity, rejection, hate, intolerance, narrow-mindedness, and deceitfulness have all slipped away. I've also learned that being misunderstood is not the end of the world; on the contrary, it is sometimes the beginning of a more in-depth emotional learning curve. I've also learned that being kind, dependable, and open-minded are exquisite skills to express and process. Heartfelt charisma, delightfulness, charm, faithfulness, confidence, and assurance is well with my soul and are also attractive attributes to develop within. As far as my "what it used to be like," grace covers a multitude of misbehaviors of myself and others.

At last, I found a liberated self and can face each day with my best self. One of the takeaways from reading this book is that the reader hopefully understands how the Spirit of Becoming leads to rebirth. One of the first books I attempted to read, published in 1936 by Dale Carnegie, was, How to Win Friends and Influence People. It was the paperback book the minister snatched from my hands as I was pacing back and forth in the church dining hall, waiting for the afternoon service to begin. I find it difficult to believe that becoming a friend is one of the first steps to change. Somehow I missed that information in Dale's book altogether.

There are recipes for empathy. I won't try to spell the measurements out to be written on an index card because I believe we each arrive at the harvest of financial humility using the same ingredients—hard work, studying, a mixture of hindsight, present sight, and foresight, known or unknown lessons to learn—which may or may not place you in the seat of empathy.

What is your process of self-forgiveness?

Part Four

The Unrestrictive Spirit

(Empowering)

"You will go out in joy and be led forth in; peace;
the mountains and hills will burst into song before you,
and all the trees of the field will clap their hands."
Isaiah 55:12 (NKJV)

The thing is–a bench can be a particular place or space to sit and ponder.

13
The Spirit of Service, Self-Love, and Laughter

An altruistic knowing of COMPETENCY

"What I know for sure is that speaking your truth is the most powerful tool we all have."

—OPRAH WINFREY

It is now 2022, and if all goes well, I will celebrate 45 years of freedom from one of the most popular elixirs in the world. Removing that from my life allowed me to look the world straight in the eye and begin to grow up. Using the spirit of service, self-love, and laughter allowed me the courage to be my best client, friend, sister, mother, employee, neighbor, and any other title a person holds.

Those around me or within other workshop environments began to point out what I was doing, and I, in turn, began to feel the service enjoyment sort of, which left me feeling good in the eyes of others. On the other hand, when I was alone, I felt just that: alone. The only thing on my mind was showing up to get another adrenaline shock, shot, or an invisible pill of outside stimulation.

I was in that class half innocently from 1977 until 1994. Soon, I had to acknowledge my truth. I recognized I no longer felt that I was serving genuinely. I begin to withdraw from the role of unconsciously and consciously impressing others. One way was the overwhelming applause. Another service manipulation was constantly being called upon to speak first and to do so exceptionally timely. The spirit of self-love and service would require much more research, work, and preparation. They forget to tell us broken ones that a self-process boot camp was a part of the change process. Therefore, I could not assist others or myself in this path of growth and development. Quickly I learned that helping others could turn into a people-pleasing proposition if boundaries aren't set.

Somewhere along the way, people pleasers decide that everyone else's needs are more pressing than their self-care. Sometimes people are glad to be hopeful about self-development and realize they have placed themselves on the back burner in their own lives and begin to feel emotionally drained, resentful, dissatisfied, and empty. As Lao Tzu says, "Care about people's approval, and you will always be their prisoner."

Another time I registered in an event, I can't recall the name exactly, but the agenda centered around rendering services on over a dozen or more business development plans. So I was again trying to broaden my territory of giving back, love, and humor.

The Spirit of Service asks, "To what extent are you willing to respect the thin line sometimes between people-pleasing and authentic serving?" Once I briefly paused to listen to Bryan Stevenson, a lawyer, giving a TED Talk. He said, "The opposite of poverty is not wealth; it is justice. I quickly thought Justice doesn't always look nor feel like justice. It looks and feels like an injustice. The value in Bryan's story was listening to him while standing on stage, reminiscing as his mother and other friends sat in their living room; retelling the story allowed me to be there briefly. I missed listening to grown folks having meaningful and healthy conversations as I grew up. I was a bit peeved because I had the complete opposite story to tell someday, yet I found myself admiring his gift of service, self-honesty, and humor.

Viktor E. Frankl has said, "When we work directly for the good of others, that is, when we engage in the spirit of service," meaning deepens in ways that reward us beyond measure.

Whenever we go beyond satisfying our personal needs, we enter the realm of what Frankl called "ultimate meaning." Some people call it a connection to a higher self, God, our spirit, universal consciousness, love, and the collective good. I call the soul of service the spirit of fellowship.

Regarding the Spirit of authentic Self-Love, everything that shamed me continued to mount yearly. I remember deciding between respect and disrespect; my father drove one of our large, unkempt trucks right in front of the school to drop me off. Sitting in the back of the filled-to-the-brim truck, I could not believe they had stopped. I was trying to decide if I should stay put or climb down the side of the tall, shabby, and raggedy truck.

At last, I concluded to climb down what seemed like at least fifteen feet to the ground. I let go. I jumped from the truck when I was safely close enough to the ground, running faster than fast into the schoolyard and on into the building. All the while, hoping no one was looking out the many classroom windows as the truck pulled up, I climbed down, and the noisy truck pulled away. I still could not believe my parents had stopped in front of the elementary school building on their way to their many work assignments for the day. Although I had never heard the word "shame," I knew the feeling significantly that day. Time crept by remorsefully; unexplained emotional, spiritual, and mental tornadoes, hurricanes, and whirlwinds became psychologically painful to be reckoned with, day by day for the next eleven years.

I felt inadequate because I could not express "Good job" to any progress I accumulated in the past 63 years when there were many expressions to encourage others and self.

I will be the first to say; that I am still learning about self-love. My knowledge is limited, but I know authentic self-love does not leave much room for operating in self-pity, shame, or wondering what others think of you. Instead, the spirit of service, self-love, and laughter is a self-sacrificing experience of competency in action.

I often asked myself, when did I recognize a life of fake laughter led nowhere? I gathered that I was looking for the spirit of authentic laughter as I continued to snatch a faint snicker here and there. Nothing seemed funny or humorous in my youth. I somehow learned consciously or unconsciously to laugh between the pain of untreated common sense and straight-up ignorance. I often wondered why it always seemed such a burden to smile, laugh, or be happy. It turned out that while surfing the web, I found a workshop that addressed the lack of laughter.

Once I arrived at the convention center, where hundreds of attendees were parading here and there at the service conference, I enthusiastically wondered what the format was for such an event. After purchasing my packet at the registration table, I slowly walked to find a seat in the enormous auditorium. It looked like everyone was over-energized. I, for one, was waiting to see and hear what the workshop was to offer.

I remembered only one thing about the event. There were large blown-up beachballs. We would hit the colorful balls back and forth across the enormous area during the intermission. It was hilarious. Lord God, I secretly hoped one of the beach balls would come to me. Finally, one did. I hit the ball so hard it flew right into someone's face; it was the funniest thing! The beach ball scene was fun. And everyone bellowed with deep belly laughter. I was not receiving anything from the speakers, just pretending to listen.

Speaking of fun and laughter, once I sponsored a social gathering. I honored the engagement to see how much fun and laughter I could digest now that I am debt-free, excluding my condo mortgage.

We created another service this past Mother's Day in 2021, the self-love and laughter segment. First, I put Michelle Obama's CD on for background listening to hear as we gathered. Secondly, I announced the plan to create Face Mask displays for Mother's Day. Thirdly, we snapped photos outside in the beautiful green and flowery scenery. I learned from that small gathering that service events do not always have to be challenging. Instead, service can be fun, self-healing, and laughter.

What service position(s) do you hold?

What are the characteristics of genuine self-love?

Can you list twenty ways laughter is a healing balm?

While sitting on the bench of more than enough, I understood that overcoming is a way of life.

14

The Spirit of Love

An Engine of Confidence

"When I let go of what I am, I become what I Might be."
—LAO TZU

Once I asked my father, what happens in the end, and you haven't found a personal savior? He said, "It doesn't happen that way." Although his remark gave me hope, it did not satisfy my phenomenon of craving for how spiritual development worked. *I learned much later; that it is not easy to imitate the fruits of the Spirit. The Spirit of love is manifested by what a person is and not just what a person does.*

I was relieved that the answer sounded hopefully promising; nonetheless, it did not supply the student with any tools to succeed forward toward the invisible quest. Although I asked that question very young, maybe about eleven or twelve, I was to see more hell and experience more hurt from that early age until I turned thirty. I was so disoriented that I could no longer look for Jesus or love. I was trying to survive by any means necessary, from miserable days to unenchanted nights repeatedly.

I did not know that receiving and giving love was a process and then an art. When I checked in to one of the world's largest and most significant treatment centers, where how to move from a spiritual illness forward toward a spirit of love, I came to believe in the powers of authentic love. I'm now learning to discern more signs and wonders along the way. One of the messages I realized was that it's a mistake to ask hurt people how to love. They can only tell you about hurt; that's all they know. I became a product of my environment where the signs of authentic love were unavailable, nonexistent, and well missed by me. I began to pass on the best information because I did not know the value of studying, learning, and developing the fruits of the spirit.

Much later in life, I accepted that I became a young lady that lived in an environment of brokenness. There were broken promises, broken homes, broken spirits of adults, disadvantaged school systems, a low non-spirit of the emptiness of church hurts, and underprivileged social connections. When you are lost and broken, it can be quite the journey to nowhere over and over year after year. So I prayed and asked the lost or misplaced God of my non-understanding for help. My search included physical, emotional, mental, spiritual, and holistic heights and valleys. The scripture for reference was Psalms 142:3 "When my spirit faints within me, you know my way!" However, the only interest I invested in was all external self-upkeep regarding clothes, hairstyles, nails, and make-up. So I became a dressed-up self-pitying lost soul.

But I began to see and take note of the people with a message of light, hope, and love. After becoming a change agent of love and happiness, I began to see what "WE" did differently when "WE" lived with love as a principal guide. We know the spirit of Love when we start to process our thoughts on a loving platform and a consistent channel.

We begin to know a new freedom.

We begin to know new happiness.

We begin to love our neighbors.

We begin to set healthy boundaries.

We begin to say "Yes," to living life on life's terms.

We begin to change the things we can more readily.

We begin to change the things we can more willingly.

We want to change and be on a higher level.

We begin to go where the brave dare not go.

We begin to see the best times today.

We begin to set worthwhile goals with intention.

We begin to act with *strength*.

We begin to move out of our way.

We begin to move out of God's way.

We begin to fear less and love more.

We begin to doubt more petite and have more faith.

We begin to walk by faith and not by sight.

We begin to walk with a new beat.

We begin to honor whose we are.

We begin to honor who we are.

We begin to understand unconditional love.

We begin to turn a blind eye to folly.

We begin to pray more.

We begin to communicate more openly.

We begin to be free to choose.

We begin to see a loving nature as a necessity.

We begin to practice letting go and moving forward.

We begin to see our imperfections as steppingstones.

We begin to reach for certainty.

We begin to feel comfortable speaking up.

We begin to overcome our fears.

We start to search for maturity.

We begin to let go of childish behaviors.

We begin to judge not that we, be not judged.

We begin to be accountable.

We begin to breathe breaths of self-confidence.

We begin to follow through with self-commitments.

We begin to let the sunshine from within.

We begin to want a better way of life.

We begin to get involved in our personal development.

We begin to enlarge our spiritual programs.

We begin to look at our faults and not theirs.

We begin to practice humility.

We begin to adopt a growth mindset.

We let love lead us closer to our purpose somehow.

We begin to lose interest in selfish things.

We begin to celebrate our wins, no matter how small.

We begin to respect our intuition.

We begin to define love as we see love.

We begin to heal from our many afflictions.

We begin to see past the inside of the box.
We can comprehend the word serenity.
We begin to want to help others.
We begin to know the difference between what is.
We begin to support our dreams and goals.
We begin to look the world in the eye.
We begin to want to follow instructions.
We begin to participate in our professional growth.
We begin to study to show ourselves.
We begin to take note of our change processes.
We begin to not lean on others as a crutch.
We begin to have wisdom.
We begin to desire a deeper divine awareness.
We gain the spirit of asking for help.
We begin to know we have choices.
We begin to fear less.
We begin have more faith.

These are some of the signs and wonders of love.

We realized we had become lost in the storms of life, and between love and grace, we found our peace and serenity. We begin to know the meaning of we come this far by faith. I started to know that there was love for the unlovable. Love lifted my spirit finally when nothing else would help. In the seventies, the love that raised me was given to me from one stranger after another.

One day I had to submit to loving the Lord God with all my heart, mind, and soul. One day, I had to commit to a life of bearing the fruit of love, and finally I had to learn how to love my neighbor as myself.

How does the spirit of love define itself in your life?

About the Author

Leona Phillips Jackson, B.A. looks forward to uncovering and discovering more knowledge concerning Spiritual Wellness and Spiritual Illness. So many of her quality skills were an ultimate surprise to Ms. Jackson, including the craft of writing. Yet, when all else failed again, she found another source of light and living through writing.

In the years ahead, Ms. Jackson will be researching uptalks about getting to know self-better: Self-Discipline, Self-Care, Self-Respect, Self-Survival, Self-Assurance, Self-Belief, Self-Trust, Self-Love, Self-Breakthroughs, Self-Amends, Self-Understanding and Forgiveness, Self-Image, Self-Praise, Self-Building, Self-Support, Self-Progress, Self-Growth, Self-Confidence, Self-Guidance, Self-Worth, Self-Wealth, and overall Self-Improvement, to learn and pass on to other self starved, and self-depleted persons.

Leona P. Jackson, B.A. is a retired Office Assistant III; from the University of Washington in Seattle, Washington. She enjoys writing and spends daily time studying. Ms. Jackson is a mom of two adult children: Richard and Secret. In addition, she is a sister to four brothers and a large number of sisters. She enjoys writing, spending, and traveling in her free time.